JERSEY 1204
A PECULIAR SITUATION

Jersey
Heritage Trust

DOUG FORD

First published Jersey 2004
By Jersey Heritage Trust, The Weighbridge, St Helier JE2 7S

Text copyright © Doug Ford 2004

Illustrations © individuals and organisations credited

Maps and line drawings © Shaun Heslop

Design by: Ross Abacus TIW

ISBN: 0-9538858-6-0

Funded by the
Education, Sport and
Culture Committee

Supported by

JERSEY 1204
A PECULIAR SITUATION

Normandy and The Channel Islands

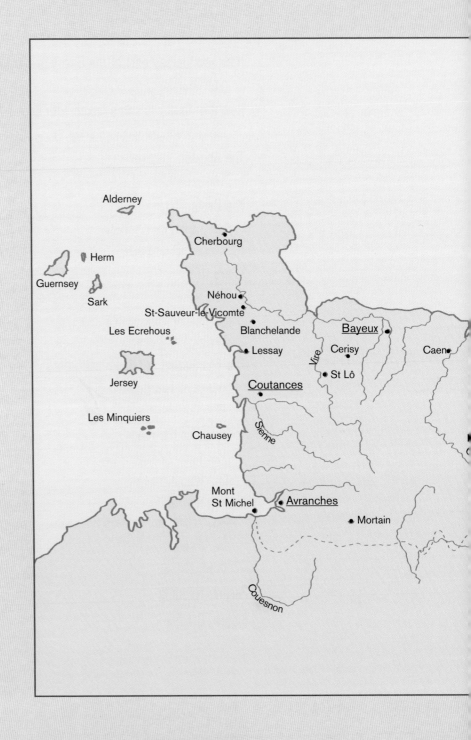

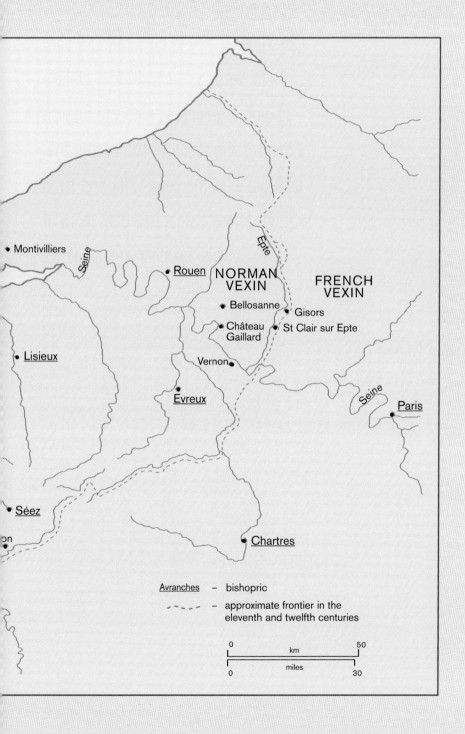

Montivilliers

Seine

Rouen

NORMAN VEXIN

Epte

FRENCH VEXIN

Bellosanne

Gisors

Château Gaillard

St Clair sur Epte

Vernon

Lisieux

Evreux

Seine

Paris

Séez

on

Chartres

Avranches – bishopric

- - - – approximate frontier in the eleventh and twelfth centuries

0	km	50
0	miles	30

6.

In 2004 Jersey is celebrating a very special anniversary because "the island's unique relationship with the English Crown is the result of the events that took place in the year 1204 and so in 2004 Jersey celebrates 800 years of this 'peculiar' relationship."

a peculiar situation

Like the other Channel Islands, Jersey was part of the old Duchy of Normandy and when the Duke defeated King Harold at the Battle of Hastings in 1066 the islands began a relationship with England that has never been really broken.

To a lot of people the islands are a bit of a mystery. British islands but not part of Great Britain, never colonies yet not part of the United Kingdom and - today - English speaking but not part of England. Jersey really is a peculiar of the Crown.

In this book we look at the origins of the links with the Duchy of Normandy, the changing role of the islands as a result of the growth of the Angevin empire and the crisis caused by John's loss of Duchy. In the century that followed, essentially during the reign of John's son, Henry III, the foundations of modern Jersey were laid down.

(1) King John of England does homage to King Philip II of France for his lands in France from the Chroniques de Saint Denis.

A Peculiar Situation **Jersey and the Duchy of Normandy**

How was Jersey part of the Duchy of Normandy?

In the ninth century invaders from Norway and Denmark began to settle in the area around the mouth of the River Seine in what we now call north-west France. Nowadays we call these men Vikings but at the time they were generally described as Northmen or Normans and the land they took became known as Normandy.

(2) The *Helge Ask* built in the Viking Ship Museum, Roskilde, Denmark is a replica of Skudelev wreck 5. It is typical of the type of ships used by William the Conqueror to transport his army over to England in 1066.

(3) How the Vikings saw themselves. A small carving on this antler found in Sigtuna, Sweden shows the head of a Viking. He is wearing a conical helmet fitted with a nasal to protect his eyes. See how well groomed his hair is and how neatly his beard is trimmed.

In 911 the French king gave one of their leaders, Hrolf Haraldsson who had the nickname of Hrolf Gangr (the Walker), the title Duke of Normandy. According to the Icelandic saga writers he was given the nickname because

". . . he was grown so big that no steed could bear him and therefore walked everywhere ..."

They also said that Hrolf began his career as a Viking because the king in Norway made him an outlaw and so he had to leave his home to make his fortune. Later writers usually referred to him as Rollo.

What had really happened was that the French king, Charles the Simple, used a band of Vikings who already held land around the mouth of the River Seine to stop other Vikings sailing up the river to attack Paris. By 911 these Viking settlers had been farming this land for about fifty years.

In 933 Rollo's son William Longsword, the second duke, captured the land in the Cotentin peninsula and the islands which had been given to the Bretons by the French in 867. Jersey had become part of the Norman world.

The western part of Normandy was the most traditionally Viking part of the duchy. The 11th century writer, Dudo of St Quentin said that although Viking speech was dead in Rouen by 1025 it was still being spoken in the area around Bayeux. The Bishop of Coutances who had been chased away from the area in the middle of the tenth century by pagan Vikings tried to return in the 990s but was unable to return until the reign of Duke Richard II in 1025.

As far as the islands were concerned they were administered by a Seneschal of Normandy, who appointed a deputy, known as the Vicomte of the Islands, to act for him on the spot. The Duke's laws were enforced by visiting judges coming over from mainland Normandy and this continued after the Norman conquest of England.

(4) Painting by Major NVL Rybot of Rollo's men arriving in Normandy.

(5) How the Vikings saw themselves. On this picture stone from the Swedish island of Gotland two Viking warriors are shown fighting with swords and carrying round shields.

The islands

There are no records of any of the Dukes of Normandy coming to visit Jersey until the winter of 1030 and even then it was an accident. In the second half of 1029 Duke Robert, the sixth duke, planned to help his cousin, Edward (later known as the Confessor) to claim the throne of England from King Cnut. He assembled a fleet to transport his army over the Channel but a storm blew up and they had to seek shelter in Jersey. Duke Robert and his men waited for a favourable wind but it never came. Greatly disappointed the duke left for mainland Normandy and called off his attack on England.

Because they were far away from the seat of power in Rouen, the islands were seen as a good place to exile trouble-makers. The seventh duke, William II (later known as William the Conqueror), sent his uncle Mauger who was Archbishop of Rouen into political exile here. With little to do, he was unable to meddle in court affairs, he seems to have spent his time between the two main islands and it was while travelling between Jersey and Guernsey that his ship was sunk in a storm and he was drowned.

Land in the island was divided up and held in return for feudal service. The local landholders held their land from larger landholders in Normandy who held their land from the Duke. This was also true of the churches; there was no major religious organisation here. They were all daughter houses to richer abbeys and monasteries on the continent.

The Dukes of Normandy *Rollo - William the Conqueror*

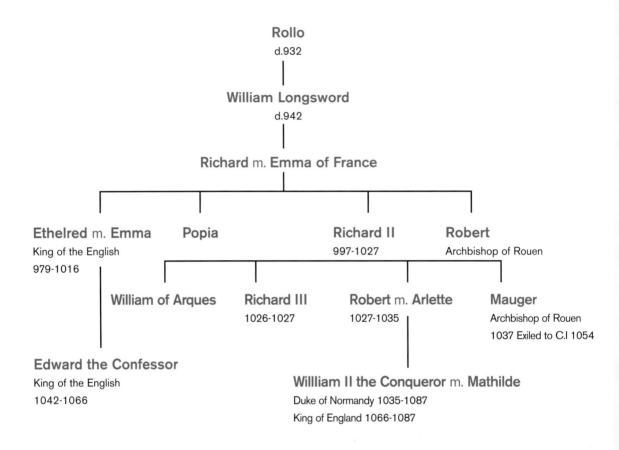

Rollo
d.932

William Longsword
d.942

Richard m. **Emma of France**

Ethelred m. **Emma**
King of the English
979-1016

Popia

Richard II
997-1027

Robert
Archbishop of Rouen

William of Arques

Richard III
1026-1027

Robert m. **Arlette**
1027-1035

Mauger
Archbishop of Rouen
1037 Exiled to C.I 1054

Edward the Confessor
King of the English
1042-1066

Willliam II the Conqueror m. **Mathilde**
Duke of Normandy 1035-1087
King of England 1066-1087

The Dukes of Normandy/Kings of England *William the Conqueror - Henry III*

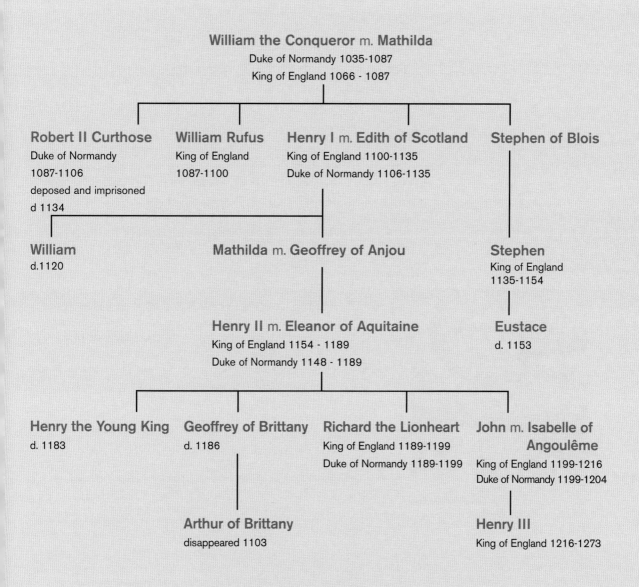

William the Conqueror m. **Mathilda**
Duke of Normandy 1035-1087
King of England 1066 - 1087

Robert II Curthose
Duke of Normandy
1087-1106
deposed and imprisoned
d 1134

William Rufus
King of England
1087-1100

Henry I m. **Edith of Scotland**
King of England 1100-1135
Duke of Normandy 1106-1135

Stephen of Blois

William
d.1120

Mathilda m. **Geoffrey of Anjou**

Stephen
King of England
1135-1154

Henry II m. **Eleanor of Aquitaine**
King of England 1154 - 1189
Duke of Normandy 1148 - 1189

Eustace
d. 1153

Henry the Young King
d. 1183

Geoffrey of Brittany
d. 1186

Richard the Lionheart
King of England 1189-1199
Duke of Normandy 1189-1199

John m. **Isabelle of Angoulême**
King of England 1199-1216
Duke of Normandy 1199-1204

Arthur of Brittany
disappeared 1103

Henry III
King of England 1216-1273

How did Jersey become linked with England?

Jersey's links with England date back to the year 1066 when Duke William II of Normandy invaded England and defeated the English King Harald Godwinsson at the Battle of Hastings.

The Jersey writer Wace, wrote about the invasion of England in his poem *Roman de Rou.* He based his story of events on his father who had seen the invasion fleet leave Normandy. It is also probable that his account of the battle was taken from people who may have taken part or certainly listened to stories by men who had been there.

William believed that he should be king of England because his cousin, Edward the Confessor, had promised him that he should succeed him in return for all the support the Normans had given him in his youth. Edward's mother had also been William's great-aunt. He also claimed that Harald Godwinsson had sworn to help him become king and this is shown in the Bayeux Tapestry which is a record of events - from the Norman point of view - leading up to William's victory at Hastings. One of the problems associated with this argument is that the English crown was elective rather than hereditary.

Nevertheless William was supported by the Pope because the Church wanted the new reforms to be brought into England and the English were resisting them.

(6) The Norman fleet approaching Pevensey, October 1066. Overleaf (7) The Normans disembarking their horses at Pevensey, October 1066.

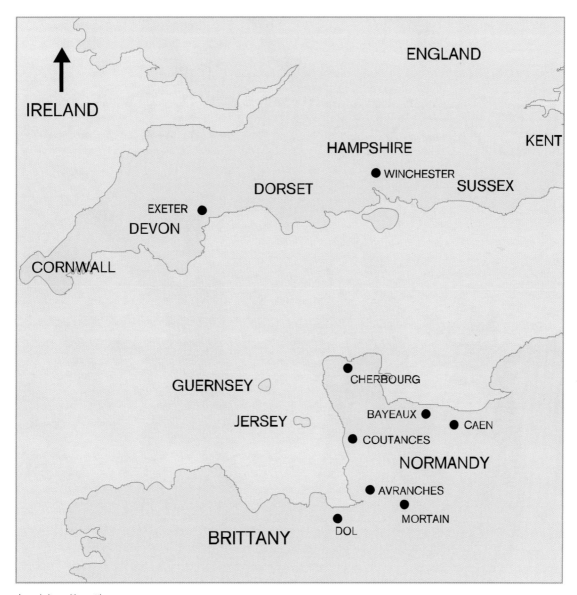

IRELAND

ENGLAND

KENT

HAMPSHIRE
● WINCHESTER

DORSET   SUSSEX

EXETER ●
DEVON

CORNWALL

GUERNSEY ◌

JERSEY ◌

● CHERBOURG

BAYEAUX ●
                    ● CAEN

● COUTANCES

NORMANDY

● AVRANCHES
                ● MORTAIN

DOL ●

BRITTANY

Jersey in its maritime setting.

A Peculiar Situation **Jersey's Links with England**

DE NAVIBVS · ET

18.

William was crowned William I, King of England, on Christmas Day 1066. The title is interesting because until this point kings had been kings of the English - the people - rather than of England - the land. William continued to be Duke of Normandy and made no attempt to join the two lands into one. When he died in 1087 he left Normandy to his eldest son Robert Curthose, who became Duke Robert II, and he left England to his second son William Rufus, who became King William II.

His third son Henry was perhaps the cleverest of his family and he managed events so well that he succeeded both his brothers and just like his father he governed the two lands separately.

(8) William with his two half-brothers Odo, Bishop of Bayeux and Robert, Count of Mortain.

Duke William of Normandy

William the Conqueror was born in the wooden castle of Falaise in Normandy in 1027 or 1028. His father was Robert "the Magnificent", the sixth Duke of Normandy and his mother was Herleve, the daughter of a rich merchant, Fulbert the Tanner. Herleve is sometimes called Arlette - this was Robert's pet name for her. Because they had been married in the old fashioned Viking way while Robert's father was duke, the Christian Church did not recognise it as legal. This was not a problem because many people were married in the "Danish fashion" and Robert had an older brother, Richard, who would succeed his father. The problem came when Richard died soon after becoming duke and Robert was his heir. Herleve was not thought to be a suitable wife for the new Duke and so she was married off to one of Richard's followers, Herluin de Conteville while her father was given the important position of chamberlain of the ducal household.

William succeeded his father as Duke in 1035 when Robert died while on a pilgrimage to the Holy Land. At first he was looked after by his great-uncle Robert, the Archbishop of Rouen, and then by a succession of guardians until he was recognised as a man in his own right and knighted by the French king, Henry I in 1042.

He married Mathilde of Flanders in 1051 and this caused a lot of trouble with the French king because he thought that Normandy and Flanders joined by marriage would threaten his western borders. Pope Leo IX was against the marriage because they were distantly related although this was really a political objection; his successor Pope Nicholas II accepted the marriage on condition that they build two churches in the city of Caen - L'Abbaye aux Hommes and L'Abbaye aux Dames.

William died on 9 September 1087 in the capital of Normandy, Rouen. He had suffered for a month, his stomach had been ruptured when he was pitched forward onto the high pommel of his saddle as he was riding through the burning streets of Mantes, near Paris. His enemies on this occasion were the King of France and his own eldest son, Robert, who was in revolt against him.

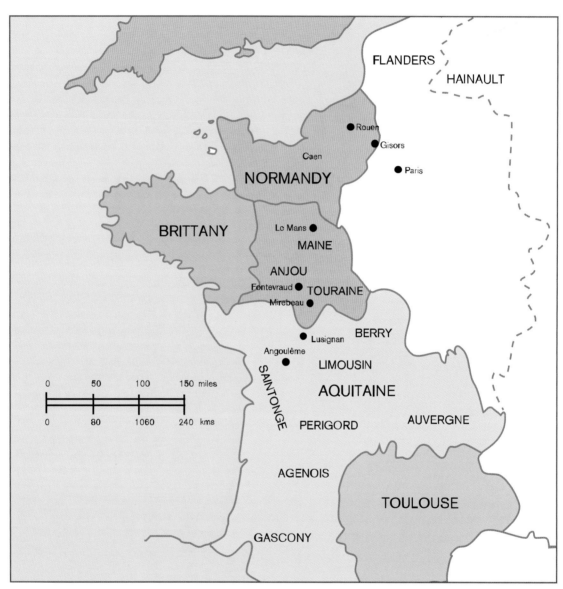

FLANDERS

HAINAULT

Rouen

Gisors

Caen

Paris

NORMANDY

BRITTANY

Le Mans

MAINE

ANJOU

Fontevraud

TOURAINE

Mirebeau

BERRY

Lusignan

Angoulême

LIMOUSIN

AQUITAINE

AUVERGNE

SAINTONGE

PERIGORD

0	50	100	150 miles
0	80	1060	240 kms

AGENOIS

TOULOUSE

GASCONY

Map of The Plantagenet Lands.

The Angevin Empire

Not all Dukes of Normandy became Kings of England after 1066. Neither were all Kings of England Dukes of Normandy.

When Henry I died in 1135 his son was already dead and the barons in England were not ready to accept his daughter Matilda as queen. Count Stephen of Blois, another one of William the Conqueror's grandchildren, whose brother Henry was Bishop of Winchester, seized the throne. While the barons in Normandy were not that keen on Stephen they were less keen on Matilda's husband, Geoffrey of Anjou.

Eventually, civil war broke out in both England and Normandy. By 1144, Geoffrey of Anjou had successfully captured Normandy and had himself declared Duke, but Stephen held on to England. When Geoffrey died in 1150, his son, Henry Plantagenet became Duke of Normandy and Count of Anjou, and four years later when Stephen died he was crowned King Henry II of England.

It was during this time that the Channel Islands began to gain some of their privileges because Geoffrey of Anjou confiscated land from those people who were loyal to Stephen and gave it to his supporters. In order to make sure the islanders stayed loyal to him he also guaranteed certain privileges and freedoms under local law - this was the beginning of trials in island courts. At the same time islanders were excused from military service outside the Channel Islands unless they were needed to go with the Duke of Normandy to recover England. Until the civil war between Stephen and Matilda there was no real need of this condition because the idea of one man ruling both countries had not really developed. Geoffrey also granted both Jersey and Guernsey the privilege of having their own Vicomte.

Key to map

▪	Inherited by Henry I
▪	Conquered by Henry II, held as a fief by Duke of Brittany
▫	Acquired by Henry II by marriage
▪	Claimed by Plantagenets as Dukes of Aquitaine

(9) The only images of the Priory building in Elizabeth Castle that exist were drawn by Wenceslaus Hollar in 1650, just before they were blown up.

In 1152 the 19 year-old Henry Plantagenet married Eleanor of Aquitaine. This shocked many people because Eleanor was 30 years old and had been married to King Louis VII of France for 15 years. Louis VII divorced her because he thought she could not have any sons. Her marriage to Henry was dangerous to the French because the young Duke of Normandy now ruled over his wife's lands in Aquitaine and Poitou which meant he controlled more of the country than the French King. Once he became King of England he would be even more powerful and throughout his reign there would be tension with the French kings.

One of the features of this new "Angevin Empire" was a growth in sea travel between the northern part of the "Empire" and the southern parts by royal servants and by merchants. As a result of this the Channel Islands became very important ports of call for ships coming from Ireland and the south coast of England en route to the Continent and for ships going around Brittany to Aquitaine.

Henry tried to encourage the island to develop and so he encouraged the foundation of an abbey dedicated to St Helier on the small tidal island in St Aubin's Bay. The actual founder was one of Henry's barons, William FitzHamon who was to become Seneschal of Nantes in 1166 and Seneschal of Brittany in 1172. The Augustinian canons who lived there acted as scribes to anyone who needed their services especially the growing numbers of merchants. It also appears that Jersey had a moneylender because in 1180 Robert, son of Vital, had to pay a fine to prevent his dead brother's goods being taken as payment of a debt resulting from a cash advance. In 1184 the Abbey was downgraded to a Priory when it was joined with the Abbey of Our Lady of the Vow in Cherbourg.

In the 13th century the shoreline at St Helier was not far from the area we now call the Parade. The Abbey was just offshore so this could have been the area of St Helier the king hoped would develop. In 1154 Henry granted the monks of the Abbey the watermill known as Le Moulin de la Ville and the area known as le Marais de St Helier; more importantly he gave them the right to establish a market. Excavations here in the early 1970s uncovered the foundations of a house which had been built in the 13th century and had stone walls and a thatched roof. The building was about 12 metres long and about 6 metres wide and was probably an aisled hall with a hearth in the centre. The space inside was divided by a partition. Amongst the finds were a coin of Henry II made by Gerrard of York around 1180-85 which was lost possibly in the first decade of the 13th century. There was also a small fragment of an early 13th century coin - possibly of Philip II Augustus.

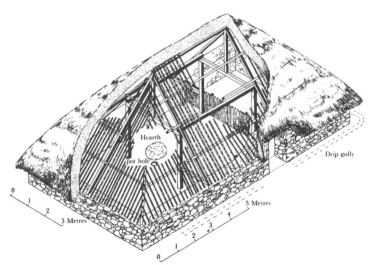

(10) Based upon the archaeological evidence the 13th century aisled hall discovered in Old Street, St. Helier may have looked like this.

(1) The tombs of Henry II and Eleanor of Aquitaine at Fontevraud Abbey..

Maistre Wace

Se l'on demande qui áo dist,	If one asks who said this,
Qui ceste estoire en romanz fist,	Who wrote this history in the vernacular,
Jo di e dirai ke jo sui	I say and will say that I am
Wace, de l'isle de Gersui,	Wace, from the island of Jersey
Qui est en mer vers occident	Which is in the sea towards the west
Al fieu de Normandie apent	And belongs to the territory of Normandy.
En l'isle de Gersui fu nez . . .	I was born on the island of Jersey . . .

During the twelfth century a leisured class eager for knowledge and entertainment grew up amongst the Norman aristocracy. Typical of their age, in that they were illiterate and unable to understand Latin, they demanded a literature in their own language and so a group of writers began to cater for their needs. A prominent figure amongst these writers was the Jerseyman, Maistre Wace who actually states that he earned his bread by writing romances.

He referred to himself as either Maistre Wace or Maistre Guace and there are no other contemporary references to him. It could be that Wace was not a surname but a shortened version of the christian name Eustache.

Wace was born in Jersey about 1100 and was sent to Caen to study and, as he described himself as a "Clerk lisant" in the reigns of three Henries, he must have been ordained before 1135 and he was still writing when Prince Henry was crowned in the reign of Henry II.

He studied in the Ile de France before returning to Caen. He may have died in 1174. Although some of his religious works still exist they tend to be translations of earlier pieces from Latin, his two most famous epic poems are the "Roman de Brut" concerning the kings of Britain and his unfinished "Roman de Rou" concerning the Dukes of Normandy.

The 16,000 line "Roman de Brut" published in 1155 is a reworking of Geoffrey of Monmouth's "History of the Kings of Britain" and starts with Brutus, the grandson of Aeneas sailing to Britain where he founded London after the fall of Troy. It continues with the story of King Lear and his daughters and the Arthurian Cycle in which Wace was the first to mention the Round Table. As a result of this work King Henry II gave him a position as one of the canons at Bayeux and commissioned him to write the Roman de Rou which he dedicated to Eleanor of Aquitaine. While he often sacrificed accuracy for the sake of a good storyline this should not detract from his skill - he was a storyteller not a journalist. His description of the events surrounding the Battle of Hastings is possibly one of the most accurate in existence as it was probably based on eyewitness accounts. Wace's epic poem of over 16,000 lines took 14 years to write and was still incomplete when he died.

(12) The exchequer building in the grounds of the castle in Caen where the taxes collected in Jersey were sent until 1204.

Several fragments of documents survive from this time which can be used to build up a view of life in the islands. It appears that in 1180 Jersey was divided up into three administrative units called ministeria - *Crapaudoit* was in the west, *Groceium* was in the centre and *Gorroic* was in the east. Each of these ministeria had their own man in charge whose job was to collect the taxes and send the money to the exchequer in Caen. These were Richard Burnouf, Roger Godel and Gislebert de la Hougue - the last was also in charge of gathering the taxes from Guernsey but he had a deputy, Robert de Haverlant, to help him. Giselbert is described as the viscomte and presiding over the royal court in Guernsey.

When Henry II died in 1189 he was succeeded as King/Duke by his eldest son Richard "the Lionheart" and it was during his reign that his youngest brother, John, was created Count of Mortain and Lord of the Isles. This meant that for the first time the Channel Islands became a distinct administrative unit. John was responsible for the government and the defence of the islands and received the revenues that would normally have gone to the duke. When John succeeded his brother as King/Duke in 1200 rather than keep the islands he made one of his Norman courtiers, Pierre de Préaux, Lord of the Isles. For the first time the Channel Islands were held by someone not from the Ducal family.

The Préaux family were minor nobility from an area just to the north-east of the Norman capital of Rouen who came to prominence during the reigns of Henry II and Richard. The Préaux connection was to have an impact on the future of the islands because when the conflict between John and Philip Augustus broke out, the family were determined not to lose the power and prestige they had gained.

The Crisis

Although John has been blamed for the loss of Normandy, it was his older brother Richard the Lionheart who did more than anyone to set the events rolling that resulted in the French King taking over the Duchy.

The French king, Philip II Augustus, had been trying to undermine Henry's position in France and supported Henry's sons whenever the family fell out. In July 1189, after years of squabbling with his sons, Henry II died at his castle in Chinon and was buried in the nearby Abbey at Fontevraud. He was succeeded by his son Richard as King/Duke. Richard and the French King, Philip II Augustus both went on a crusade to free the Holy Places from the Muslims. They were supposed to share any wealth they made in the adventure but soon fell out when Richard announced that he was going to marry Berengaria of Navarre the daughter of King Sancho VI instead of Philip's sister Alice. Philip told Richard that if he did marry Berengaria then they would be enemies for the rest of their lives. Even though they did go to Palestine to fight the crusade and recover the Holy Places, Philip soon returned to France in disgust at Richard's behaviour.

(13) Both sides of the seal of King John.
On one side, surrounding the image of the King on his throne, the inscription reads "The King of England, the Lord of Ireland" while on the other he shown as a mounted knight and the inscription reads "Duke of Normandy and Aquitaine, Count of Anjou".

Richard's army failed to capture Jerusalem and he eventually returned to Aquitaine and Normandy where he began to build a great castle - Château Gaillard at Les Andelys - which could control the river Seine. This was despite an earlier treaty between the King of France and the Duke of Normandy which had specifically forbidden the building of a castle on this site. Philip invaded Normandy but was beaten in a battle at Gisors and as they retreated Richard had the pleasure of watching him fall off his horse into the River Epte.

(14) Attacking a castle - a detail from the Maciejowski Bible. c.1240.

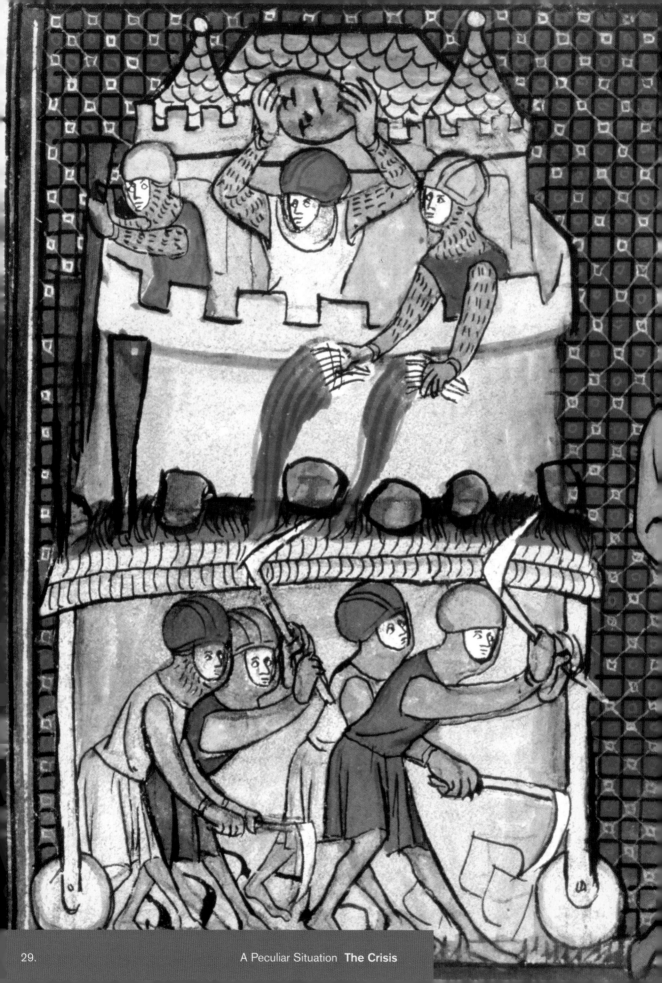

A Peculiar Situation **The Crisis**

In a letter to the bishop of Durham, Richard said

"Thus we have defeated the King of France ...; but it is not we who have done the same, but rather God and our right (Dieu et mon droit)..."

It is from this letter that the English Crown adopted *Dieu et mon droit* as its motto. The war carried on and it was while he was attacking a castle at Chalus, near Limoges, in 1199 that Richard was killed by an arrow.

This brought the question of the succession out into the open. With England, Normandy and Aquitaine accepting Richard's youngest brother John as ruler while the nobility of Brittany, Anjou and Maine supported Richard's nephew, Arthur. This, of course, drove a wedge between the areas loyal to John, and Philip was not slow to exploit the situation to strengthen his position and to reassert his authority in those parts of France. In 1202 he invaded Normandy in support of Arthur's claim.

Arthur had invaded the disputed land from the west and was laying siege to the castle of Mirabeau, in the hope of taking his grandmother, Eleanor of Aquitaine, hostage when John made a superb, forced march instead and captured the Bretons totally unaware. Arthur was taken prisoner and was never seen alive again. Rumours flew that John had ordered him killed.

Whatever the truth of the matter, his death certainly made the struggle easier to understand, the conflict was simply between Philip Augustus and John. The French invaded Normandy and John withdrew before them. Many of the landowners went over to the French side and one by one the castles in Normandy surrendered. John was in danger of losing Normandy, yet in December 1203 he left Rouen to spend Christmas in England. A French army laid siege to the fortress of Château Gaillard which controlled the River Seine leading up to Paris and by the end of March 1204 the English garrison surrendered. Three months later, Pierre de Préaux surrendered John's main town in Normandy - Rouen. The Duchy had been lost and it seemed that the Channel Islands were taken over by the pro-French faction.

The situation in the islands appears to be confused. When Pierre de Préaux surrendered Rouen he also had to pay homage to Philip Augustus for all his land in Normandy and this included the Channel Islands. According to the *Romance of Eustace the Monk*, John sent a naval force of thirty galleys under Eustace to recapture the islands in the summer of 1205. The leader of the islands was a man called Romeril. The following year John sent another fleet of five galleys and three great ships manned by 275 men across to the islands where, once John's authority had been re-established, Hasculf de Suligny, lord of Combourg was appointed to govern in Jersey, and Geoffrey de Lucy to govern Guernsey. Finally separated from the rest of Normandy a new form of island government gradually developed. De Suligny was suspicious of the islanders and so in order to make sure that they remained loyal to King John he took hostages from all the leading families. These were sent to England with the threat that if their families should prove to be disloyal they would be executed. He also started to build a castle on the east coast of Jersey and another in the middle of St Peter Port harbour.

Even though he had taken hostages, De Suligny did not want to upset the islanders more than he needed to. There was no attempt made to change the old laws and introduce English laws probably because John hoped he would recapture Normandy some day. The Church still remained linked to the diocese of Coutances and the various churches in the islands were daughter houses of larger monasteries in Normandy. However, he did get rid of the three administrative divisions in Jersey and replace them with one central control. It was about this time that the role of jurats began to develop in the islands.

When hostilities broke out once more in 1212, the islands were raided by Eustache who had changed sides. This time the story was different as the islands were defended with castles and there was a nucleus of professional soldiers. Beaten back from Jersey and Guernsey, a small band of his followers settled on Sark in 1212 from where they mounted pirate attacks on island shipping. They were eventually defeated in 1214 when Philip d'Aubigny and a force of Jerseymen recovered the island and sent the prisoners to Winchester. This action resulted in the King returning the hostages he had taken eight years

earlier because he was now convinced of the loyalty of the islanders.

In England many of the Barons resented John's high handed actions and this eventually led to a revolt by some of the Barons. The first stage ended in 1215 with King John signing a Great Charter - *Magna Carta* - which was sort of an agreement of rights between the King and his followers. However, nothing improved and the second phase ended with the Barons appealing to the French king for military help and John recalled d'Aubigny from the Channel Islands. While this was happening, over the Channel Eustache mounted another attack on the islands and, according to the Prior of Dunstable, Jersey was captured.

Just when it looked as if the islands would become French the situation was resolved when King John died at Newark on October 18th 1216 leaving his nine-year-old son Henry III, king of England. The Barons returned to their allegiance to the English throne and the French army in England led by the Dauphin[1], Prince Louis, was stranded. A French relief force led by Eustache was defeated at sea by an English naval force led by Philip d'Aubigny off the coast near Dover. Eustache was captured and immediately executed by having his head chopped off over the side of the ship. As part of the agreement with the French securing the safe return of the Dauphin and his army the Channel Islands had to be given back.

While all this was going on, in the Channel Islands there was evidence of quite a large scale trade in dried fish. The Duke, or the seigneurs to whom he had granted the privilege, supplied land near the seashore where fishing boats could land their catch and spread it out on wooden drying frames called "esperkeria". The fishermen had to use these and pay for the right to use them. In 1199 the Duke's esperkeria in the islands earned him at least 50 *livres angevins*. It was not only islanders who used them. In 1195 Vitel de Biele of Bayonne in Gascony leased the Channel Islands fisheries from Richard the Lionheart. The main catch was conger and mackerel which were preserved by salting them which in turn meant that large amounts of salt had to be brought into the islands from Gascony and the Vendeé.

[1] Dauphin was the title given to the eldest son and heir of the King of France.

King John and Arthur

John who was born in Oxford on Christmas Eve 1167 was the youngest of
Henry II and Eleanor of Aquitaine's children. He was known as Lackland
because by the time he was born his father had already decided how his lands
should be divided on his death. In an attempt to create an inheritance for
himself John was sent to the area around Dublin in Ireland known as the
Pale. Unable to defeat the Irish he was then named Softsword because of his
lack of military experience. Always his father's favourite, John is said to have
broken Henry's heart when he joined the rebellion against him in 1189. Like
his older brothers John always put self-interest first and when his brother
Richard was away on Crusade he tried to take the Crown. Later, this was to
be used as the background to many of the Robin Hood stories. When Richard
died as a result of a wound at Chalus his nephew Arthur of Brittany probably
had a better claim to the throne but it was John who succeeded him in
England and Normandy. Arthur was the son of John's older brother Geoffrey
and Constance of Brittany. He was only 12 years of age and was regarded as
too young and inexperienced to handle such a large holding.

John's marriage to Isabelle of Angouléme in 1200 was the immediate cause
of the breakdown in relations between John and the French King, Philippe
Augustus. Isabelle was already betrothed to Hugh de Lusignan, Count de La
Marche, one of John's main landholders in Poitou. Because he refused to pay
compensation, Hugh took his case against John before the king of France and
John refused to attend. The French king saw this as an opportunity to get rid
of Plantagenet power in France and so in early 1202 he announced that John
had broken his feudal obligations. The price of this was that John was to lose
his lands in France - the French king was to have Normandy and the rest of
John's French possessions were to be given to Arthur. The stage was set for a
show down.

(16) Effigy of King John. Having lost most of his
continental lands, John was buried in Worcester
Cathedral.

Eustace the Monk

Eustace 'the Monk' was actually a pirate and an outlaw! He was so famous that he had a story written about him. The oldest version of the story we have today was written about 1284 and we think the text was originally written in the late 1220s in the area around Boulogne in northern France. Eustache came from Courset in Picardy and as a young man spent some time in the Mediterranean around Italy. He returned home and became a Benedictine monk in the monastery of St Vulmar near Boulogne. The religious life did not suit him and he was soon known as the 'black monk'. His biography describes him teaching the other monks bad language and losing the monastery's crucifixes and jewels whilst gambling in local taverns.

He left the monastery about 1190 when his father was murdered. Eustace identified the killer as Hainfrois de Heresinghen and challenged him to a trial by combat. Both Eustace and Hainfrois nominated champions to fight on their behalf but in the end Eustace's champion was beaten and, as a result, Hainfrois was found not guilty. Eustace next appears as Seneschal to Renaud, Count of Boulogne in 1204. However, his dispute with Hainfrois did not end with the trial. It is likely that Eustace was forced to leave his job with Renaud after Hainfrois accused him of mismanagement. Indeed, Renaud became a more powerful enemy than Hainfrois and Eustace soon found himself living as an outlaw in the forests around Boulogne whilst conducting a guerrilla campaign of disruption and theft against the Count. He eventually fled to England having escaped justice at the hands of Philip Augustus, the King of France.

In January 1205, Eustace appeared in England and presented himself to King John. It was a profitable move for Eustace who shortly found himself commanding thirty of John's galleys, possibly with the aim of recovering Normandy for the English. Eustace and his crew of Flemish, English and even French sailors soon began attacking the coasts of Normandy.

Eustace's biography is a valuable source of information on the history of the Channel Islands in the years after 1205. By September of that year, Eustace led the military forces which King John had provided, into the Channel Islands and expelled the occupying French forces.

During the battle to regain the Islands, Eustace is described as a fearsome fighter.

'Then a great melee began, savage, violent and arduous, and Eustace held a savage axe with which he struck great blows on the battlefield. He splintered many a helmet and many a warhorse lost its shoulder. He struck blows to the right and blows to the left, making himself lord and master of the fighting. Eustace said, 'Go to it! You'll soon see them take flight'. There was a great and fierce battle there and that day many biers had to be constructed. Eustace threw everyone out of the islands, which he destroyed with the result that there was nothing left to burn in either castle or dwelling'.

Once he had secured the islands for John, Eustace was sent an additional force of five galleys and three 'great ships' with 275 seamen on board. These were to head a campaign against the French mainland. Meanwhile Eustace established a base for himself on Sark. It is unclear how he spent the next few years but about 1212 he switched allegiance back to the French king Philip Augustus. In 1214 he was forced from Sark by the Warden of the Isles, Philip d'Aubigny , who captured Eustace's brother and uncle and several knights. D'Aubigny ordered that they should be made to pay for their own food whilst held in prison.

Eustace certainly rose quickly in the ranks of the French Navy. When Prince Louis sailed across the English Channel in 1216 to claim the English throne, he travelled in Eustace's own ship. They were accompanied by a large fleet of seven or eight hundred vessels which Eustace had assembled personally. The attack was eventually repelled but another campaign was soon mounted by the French in 1217. Eustace left Calais on 23rd of August that year to escort a convoy of supplies to the French forces in England but was attacked in what has become known as the battle of Sandwich. Their tactic of throwing powdered lime into the faces of the French proved successful. Eustace's ship was boarded by the English who immediately beheaded him. They clearly did not want to take any chances with Eustace or give him any opportunity to escape from them.

(17) A Castle under Attack, a detail from the Maciejowski Bible. c. 1240.

34.

(18) Anointing of the King - a detail from the Maciejowski Bible. c.1240.

Henry III

In 1218 Henry III wrote

"It is not our intention to institute new assizes in the islands at present, but it is our will that the assizes which were observed there in the time of King Henry our grandfather, King Richard our uncle, and of the Lord King John our father, should be observed there now"

The following year the Warden, Philip d'Aubigny, collected *the fouage* - a hearth tax - for the king. This continued the practice from the times of the Dukes of Normandy and was intended to give the islanders the impression of continuity in order to ensure their loyalty. At the same time he ordered an inquest into the loyalty of the chief islanders. The result of this was that there was a redistribution of land as some tenants had their land confiscated on suspicion of disloyalty and others who proved to be more friendly to the cause received more land. From this upheaval the De Carterets emerged as the main island family - it is perhaps not surprising as they had married into the d'Aubigny family. As a result of these changes a new set of ruling families emerged in the islands drawn from the king's officials and from the minor landholders who saw the chance to get rid of their old feudal superiors. It is not surprising that the authorities should remain suspicious of people in the islands because of the fact that the islands were a way-point on the long sea route to Gascony, and they could also be used as a jumping off point for any re-conquest of Normandy. In 1223 a rule was made that any landowner who spent more than a week in Normandy would have his estates confiscated. This was because of the fear that they may have been plotting an invasion.

(19) Detail from the Lutrell Psalter showing an archer spanning a crossbow using a belt hook.

(20) The Seal of Philip d'Aubigny.

The King's Authority

Following the separation, any documents requiring the King's authority had to be sent to England for the Royal Seal to be attached to it and in times of war or even in bad weather this could be a dangerous affair. The seal was important and showed three things:

- *the source of the document or object to which it was attached.*

- *the contents had not been tampered with if it had been used to close something up (seal it). And most importantly*

- *it demonstrated authenticity because if your seal appeared on a document you were bound to honour the contents, but also, something without a seal could be regarded as void.*

Edward I gave a seal to the islands in 1279 after some deeds were lost at sea while en route to Westminster. The seal carried the royal arms of the three lionized leopards of England surrounded by a Latin inscription which meant "Seal of the Bailiwick of the Isles for the King of England".

In 1254 Henry III of England and Alfonso X of Castille signed the Treaty of Toledo and one of the conditions was that Henry's son, Prince Edward (later Edward I), was to marry Alfonso's sister Elinor of Castille. Edward was given Gascony and went to live there. At the same time he was put in charge of the Channel Islands with the title 'Lord of the Isles'. He had two bailiffs under him, one in Jersey and one in Guernsey. At this time the French were developing the idea of France as a nation and the King, Louis IX, defined the Kingdom of France as being the old Roman province of Gaul rather than just the kingdom of the Franks. He changed the civil law to state that the King had the right to demand services from his sub-vassals regardless of the wishes of their immediate lord. They were to serve the public good in the name of the country (patrie) which was defined not as the region but of the kingdom. Louis forbade private war and consolidated his power in the lands he controlled by making sure that all aggression was channelled for the good of the state.

In England, on the other hand, Henry was in dispute with his barons who were pushing for more power. The English barons led by Simon de Montfort were applying pressure on the King who tried to resolve his international problems in order to concentrate on the domestic situation. In October 1259 Henry signed the Treaty of Paris in which he gave up his claims to the regions of Normandy, Maine, Anjou and the other lost Angevin territories and Prince Edward had to pay homage to Louis IX for Gascony. In return, he did get two regions just to the north of Gascony - Perigord and Quercy. Really, the Treaty of Paris simply acknowledged the situation on the ground as the French already controlled Normandy, Anjou, Maine, and Touraine and Henry controlled the Perigord and Quercy. However, by the treaty, Henry III secured his southern possessions and strengthened his position in Gascony with its all-important wine revenues.

In late 1272, after 56 years on the throne, Henry III died: he was succeeded by his son Edward I. Edward's very good friend, Otho de Grandison was made Warden of the Isles and then given the title of Lord of the Isles which he held for over 50 years during which time he was sent to Gascony to put down rebellions on three occasions, he was sent as Edward's ambassador to the Papal Court seven times and spent six years on a Crusade. It is hardly surprising that de Grandison was nearly 90 before he actually came to the islands.

(21) Detail from the Lutrell Psalter showing an archer stringing a longbow using his foot hook.

Wars with the French

As far as the French authorities were concerned once the Channel Islands were separated from mainland Normandy and became associated with England they represented a military threat right on their own doorstep. As a result of this, the islanders had to be constantly on their guard for French invasions. At the same time the islands were used as a jumping off point by English forces whenever hostilities against France were planned. In 1214 King John sent three galleys to protect the islands and ten years later, in 1224, his son, Henry III sent two great ships, ten boats and ten sorneccas to protect the islands. By this time the French king, Louis VIII had captured the port of La Rochelle and so threatened the trade between Bordeaux and Southampton. This meant that every war between England and France would be fought at sea as well on land.

There must have been some ships permanently based in the islands because in 1243 the Warden, Drew or Drogo de Barentin was ordered to meet the King who was sailing up from Bordeaux to England. He was to sail off the coast of Brittany with "as many galleys and other good vessels" as he could gather to escort the Royal party across the Channel.

While Edward I was more concerned with his wars in Wales and in Scotland there was an incident in 1294 when the men of Dover imagined they had been insulted by Norman seamen, issued a challenge, and in the ensuing fight off the coast of Brittany won a great victory. To avenge this the French launched a raid on the Channel Islands: the islands were unprepared and suffered great damage. In Jersey over 1,500 islanders were killed, houses were burned, churches robbed and animals slaughtered. Help was sent but the islanders complained of their treatment from Otho de Grandison and the result was that the King ordered an inquiry into the state of affairs in the islands.

The main periods of war
with France were

1202-06	1230	1324-25
1212-17	1242-43	1337 (the Hundred Years war began)
1224-27	1294-1303	

In addition to these there were occasional raids in periods of heightened international tension such as the 1336 raid by David Bruce, King of Scotland.

Philip d'Aubigny

The d'Aubigny family came from the area of Brittany around Combourg. Philip first appears in Robert of Leicester's entourage in the 1190s and then as a member of King John's court. In 1207 he took over from Robert de Lacy in Guersney and Alderney and in 1212 he became governor of Jersey as well, when he took over from his friend Hasculf de Suligny. He appointed his brother Oliver to be his deputy whose daughter married Philip de Carteret, the Seigneur of St Ouen.

(22) Tomb of Philip D'Aubigny in Jersuslaem.
The de Carteret family was linked by marriage to d'Aubigny and so took his coat of arms.

Key to map

Priories

H+ Conventual Priory of St. Helier of the Islet (dependent of the abbey of Notre-Dame du Voeu, Cherbourg)

MSM+ Priory of the abbey of Mont Saint Michel

SSV+ Priory of the abbey of Saint-Sauveur-le-Vicomte

Patrons of Parish Churches

BI Abbot of Blanchelande

BP Bishop of Coustances

CE Abbot of Cerisy

CH Abbot of Notre-Dame du Voeu, Cherbourg

L Abbot of Lessay

MSM Abbot of Mont Saint-Michel

SSV Abbot of Saint-Sauveur-le-Vicomte

The Foundation of Island Institutions

Once the initial uncertainty surrounding the fate of the islands was settled, John was faced with two choices - he could absorb the islands into his realm of England or he could treat them as a separate and distinct unit. He chose the second course as he still harboured ambitions to retake Normandy and continued to treat the islands as if they were still part of the Duchy and this continued even after Henry III gave up the title of Duke of Normandy in 1259. This general policy of keeping the islands as far as possible in the state they were before the loss of Normandy is sometimes called the *"status quo ante bellum"* . In 1856 CT Le Quesne in his Constitutional History of Jersey wrote:

"They (the islands) belonged to the Crown, they formed no part of the realm."

In other words they were a possession of the King of England but were not part of his Kingdom. This meant that the links with England were through the person of the king and so an alternative administrative and legal framework had to be set up for the islands. The result was that John and his successors were represented in the islands by wardens - if they were appointed for life they were referred to as Lords of the Isles but if they were appointed for a set term then they were called Wardens.

Wardens and Lords

The Wardens were royal servants, never islanders, and as such did not usually live in the islands. In fact they only had to be here to preside over the assizes, which according to the old Norman custom had been held every three years by visiting justices. However, as the Wardens often had other duties in Brittany or Gascony the islands were a useful stopping off point on their journeys to and from England. As the king's representatives in the islands these Lords and Wardens were responsible for exercising the king's authority at a military, a judicial and an administrative level. They had to collect royal taxes and revenues, and to look after the castles and the defences of the islands which meant they were often referred to as the Keeper of the Castles or as Captain of the Royal Garrisons.

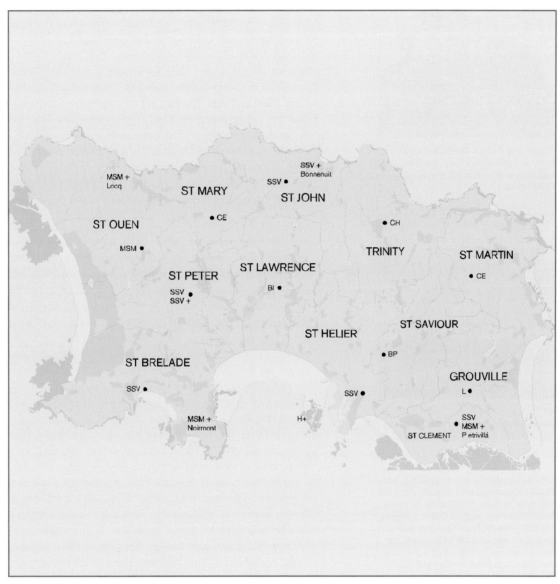

Map of the Parishes in Jersey and their mother houses

(23) The Abbot of Mont St Michel whose own Abbey was on the frontier between Normandy and Brittany had large estates in the island as well as on the nearby Cotentin peninsula.

(24) The Abbot of Cerisy-la-Forêt, near Bayeux, was patron of the churches of St Mary and St Martin. They were given to the abbey by William the Conqueror.

(25) - Right The west facade of the cathedral of Saint-Sauveur in Coutances cathedral, Normandy -Jersey had been part of the diocese of Coutances for many years before 1204 and even though the Wardens confiscated land from members of the pro-French party in the island, Jersey remained so until the Reformation over three centuries later. The cathedral was the headquarters of the church administration in the region and clergy and layman travelled between the islands and Coutances on church business.

As the Wardens were absent so often the work must have been done by deputies who are sometimes referred to as *ballivi*. These were the men on the ground who carried out the royal administration of the islands and as such were seen as important within the island communities. Their appointment was a useful source of patronage and because the practicality of the matter demanded that they should be resident in the islands they were usually islanders. These *ballivi* had to take on all sorts of royal duties but perhaps the most important was the holding of sessions of the royal court in between the assizes. This royal court was the manorial court for the royal domain and the seigneural court for the tenants-in-chief and by the end of the century had three principal sessions each year. The position of the modern Bailiff having the responsibility for the administration of royal justice can also be identified by the end of the 13th century.

The law before the separation of 1204 had been that of Normandy but this obviously had to be modified. In 1248 the Warden, Drogo de Barentin, was ordered by Henry III to set down the customs and rights enjoyed by the islanders in case disputes should spring up between the islanders and the Wardens. It was then the so called "Constitutions of King John" first appeared - in it, islanders claimed that John had granted the islands certain rights. Of the eight 'constitutions' all but the first two refer to the security of the islands, and the regulation of commerce and fishing. The first 'constitution' refers to the islanders right to be judged in their own island by 12 jurats unless they had to appeal to the king, and they also won the right that all fines and penalties would be decided by these jurats. In Jersey and Guernsey the number of jurats was set at 12, while in Alderney it was 7 and in Sark it was 6. The fact that these jurats were drawn from local landholders meant that they would know the laws and customs of the islands. The second 'constitution' allowed islanders to begin an action in the royal court without having to obtain the king's permission first and this could be heard by the resident *Ballivus* (Bailiff) without having to wait the arrival of the visiting assize justices.

The first reference to the bailiff is in the Constitutions of King John set down in 1248 in which he was described as the King's Coroner and President of the Royal Court. Gradually the role of tax collector disappears. In 1279 the bailiff in Jersey and in Guernsey were each given their seals and by the end of the century the position of bailiff had become permanent.

(26) From its hurried start in the years following 1204, Mont Orgueil developed into one of the major strongholds in the region.

A Peculiar Situation **The Foundation of Island Institutions**

The Conclusion

When Henry III of England and Louis IX of France signed the Treaty of Paris in 1259 the two kings recognized that possession of land was really the only thing that mattered in determining title. So, those parts of France occupied by the Capetian kings were recognised as being French and the Channel Islands did not fall into this category.

The islands held an enormous strategic advantage to the English kings as they were on the route to Gascony in south west France and after 1259 they began to be regarded as a valuable link between these two parts of the Royal domain. The fact that they remained loyal to John and his heirs rather than, along with the rest of Normandy, joining with the French king must mean that, in general, some of the leading islanders saw it to their advantage. The result of this new situation was that island landholders lost their old feudal superiors on the continent and gained a new and higher social, political and legal status as tenants-in-chief because of it: they now held their land directly from the Crown. Whereas this situation would usually have meant heavy military responsibilities or financial obligations the new island "aristocracy" were excused these because of their position as frontier posts on the edge of a potential war-zone.

King John and his successors had the foresight to allow the islanders to keep their Norman identity and heritage and to allow contact with mainland Normandy where many of them had relatives. The Church, of course, was of great assistance in all of this because the island remained in the diocese of the Bishop of Coutances, and would do so until the middle of the 16th century, and island churches had Norman mother houses.

The results of the events of 1204 are still with us, for the Channel Islands today are the result of decisions taken at that time. Choices made by islanders then and the institutions forced on them by feudal rulers have resulted in the rather peculiar position the islands hold - neither part of the United Kingdom nor have they ever been a colony, loyal to the Crown but not a Crown Dependency and never represented in the Westminster Parliament.

Over 800 years they have evolved into the small independent islands they are today but the political and constitutional foundations of modern Jersey were laid by the time Henry III gave up his claim to the title of Duke of Normandy in 1259.

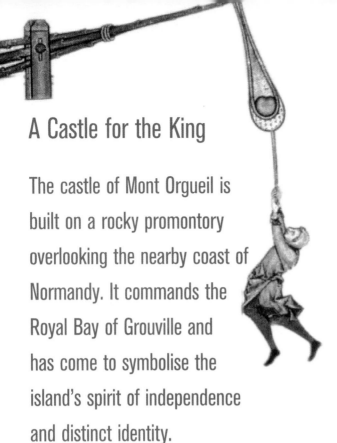

A Castle for the King

The castle of Mont Orgueil is built on a rocky promontory overlooking the nearby coast of Normandy. It commands the Royal Bay of Grouville and has come to symbolise the island's spirit of independence and distinct identity.

Until 1204 there was no need of a castle in Jersey; the Channel Islands were a peaceful backwater far from the seat of ducal power. This all ended when the French king, Philip II Augustus, captured Rouen and Plantagenet rule in Normandy was ended. For two years the Duchy had been split between different groups supporting the French king and the Norman duke, John, who also happened to be King of England and Duke of Aquitaine. The Channel Islands took the opportunity to remain loyal to their Duke and so began their long but peculiar relationship with the Crown of England. The biggest change in the Channel Islands was that they were no longer a peaceful backwater and became potential frontier posts on the edge of a war-zone. In order to protect the islands a castle had to be built. Obviously, the place to build a castle was in St Peter Port, Guernsey with its deep-water harbour although when it came to threatening France the east coast of Jersey was better.

The first documentary sources we have for the castle in Jersey was a letter dated November 1212 in which King John ordered Hasculf de Suligny to hand over the island and the castle to Philip d'Aubigny. Garrisons were sent to both islands and a building programme was started.

(27) Reconstruction of how Gorey Castle may have looked from the sea.

(28) Reconstruction of how Gorey Castle may have looked from the East.

A Peculiar Situation **A Castle for the King**

The site chosen in Jersey had been used as a defensive place since the Iron Age and possibly as early as the Neolithic period. The earth rampart and ditch would have been degraded but would have provided a good start for the new fortress which was built on the rocky ridge.

The shape of the stone buildings was determined by the narrowness of the ridge with a hall being connected to two square towers by long passageways. Access to the hall was through an enclosed staircase. The area inside the ramparts below was further strengthened in 1224-5 when 1,000 tree trunks were sent to the islands from the New Forest to make palisades for the two new castles. In addition Jersey also received five cartloads of lead, the timber from 20 oak trees and 60 bags of nails to assist with the building.

Once it was built, the castle served as the base for the garrison which was often recruited from the mainland and maintained by the King's representative, the Keeper, from the Crown revenues. The Close Rolls of Henry III contain many references to arms, shields and coats of mail being shipped to the castle garrison from Southampton and the Tower of London along with mention of cargoes of timber, beams and lead. There are also numerous entries made by the English Treasury for work and repairs carried out in the castle. The castle acquired a circuit of walls and round towers at this time and in the 1250s the "bridge of the King's Castle" is repaired.

(29) A copy by Major NVL Rybot of a 14th century original manuscript showing Bertrand du Guesclin attacking a castle.

The later Middle Ages

As with many castles, work on maintaining fortifications was neglected in times of peace and so in the summer of 1294 the island was caught unprepared when a French fleet commanded by John d'Harcourt and Matthew de Montmorency mounted a massive raid, laid waste to the island and according to a petition to the King over 1,500 islanders were killed. The castle was not taken although the keeper, Sir Henry de Cobham does not appear to have taken any real steps to protect the island as the garrison, commanded by Reginald de Carteret, was seven serjeants and they had not received any pay despite the fact that de Cobham had collected the revenues.

In 1327 Sir John des Roches was sent to the Channel Islands to inspect and strengthen defences, and the following year he was appointed Keeper. It was probably during his term of office that Grosnez Castle on the island's northwest corner was built. At Gorey he strengthened the defences and built a large tower to the north of the Keep which was to be known as the Rocheford. When he arrived he found the garrison to be made up of 3 men-at-arms drawing 12d a day, a constable and his attendant drawing 6d a day and 30 foot soldiers drawing 2d. This was obviously a time of international tension because a number of Jersey vessels were attacked by the French and their crews killed and there had been an attack on Guernsey. In his report to the King, des Roches said that the castle had been partly in ruins, under equipped and the garrison had not been paid. In his report he set out a defence plan in which he said that the best way to defend the island was for the ordinary defence of the island to be left in the hands of the ordinary people - and the castle to be maintained and manned by an English garrison.

In his reports des Roches refers to repairing damage to the buildings in the castle which had been caused by a great wind. He also describes rebuilding the decaying walls and names different parts of the castle - the chapel, the pantry, the kitchen, the bakehouse, the prison, houses, turrets and walls. There are also references to roofing the buildings and remaking the bridge. The peacetime garrison is set down as 30 men.

(30) A reconstruction of the front gate of Grosnez Castle.

When the Hundred Years War broke out the island was well protected, the castle was revictualled and garrisoned with archers and other infantry. In 1337 the Constable of the Castle was the Seigneur of Rozel, John de Barentin, and he had a garrison of 80 men which was increased to 94 the following year and he had 8 men-at-arms. This was the situation when on 26th of March Sir Nicholas Behuchet landed his French army in Jersey. They spent the summer laying waste to the island and besieging the castle, on 10th September de Barentin was killed whilst leading his men in a sortie. The siege was finally lifted in the late autumn when the French returned to Normandy before winter settled in. A second expedition was sent to capture Guernsey which they held until October 1340 when an English expedition lead by Walter de Weston recaptured it although they did hold on to Castle Cornet until 1345.

In 1339 Sir Robert Bertram, Lord of Briquebec and Marshall of France who had been granted Guernsey by the French King arrived to take up his possession which also included Jersey. Accompanied by Nicolas Helie and a large number of barons, the French had a fleet of 35 ships from Normandy and 17 Genoese galleys. The new Constable of the Castle was Sir Reginald de Carteret and he had a garrison of 12 men-at-arms, 6 armoured men, 136 crossbow-men and 117 archers. The island militia had been reorganised in 1337 into companies of thousands, one hundreds and twenties by the Keeper, Thomas de Ferrers. This militia was obviously effective because the French spent a little time burning and pillaging but left the island by March 12th 1339. Because Castle Cornet was still in the hands of the French, the King continued to maintain a strong garrison in Jersey. An entry for 1341 has the garrison making brattices [2].

In 1369 a new threat emerged and so further work was carried out on repairing and consolidating the castle. In 1372 Ivan of Wales mounted a raid on Guernsey. The Keeper of Jersey and Constable of the Castle, Edmund Rose, enlisted twenty men-at-arms and twenty archers to the Jersey garrison and the following year when he was replaced by William de Asthorp the King had ordered the Sheriffs of Plymouth and Southampton to hold ships in readiness for the transport of soldiers, horses, victuals, supplies and munitions. In 1373 Bertrand du Guesclin attacked the island in late July and laid siege to the castle. He went for the fast approach to siege warfare and by concentrating his firepower on one part of the castle he managed to breach the outer ward walls. The garrison retired to the inner parts of the castle and rather than carry on with a war of attrition negotiated a position whereby if the castle was not relieved by English troops by Michaelmas in late September they would surrender to the French. This allowed du Guesclin to return to Brittany leaving only a small garrison in the island.

Although a relief force from England did save the day the weakness of the island's defences had been highlighted and during 1374 and 1375 the French kept raiding the island. Du Guesclin was able to make the islanders pay a ransom each year in order to prevent him unleashing his forces.

In July 1403 the Breton fleet commanded by Admiral de Penhouet attacked Jersey and while the castle held out, the island suffered badly. Little is known of the castle in the early 15th century although traditionally it received the name Mont Orgueil from the Duke of Clarence, brother of Henry V. During the Wars of the Roses Margaret of Anjou, wife of Henry VI, negotiated with her cousin Pierre de Brezé, Comte de Maulevrier, and Grand Seneschal of Normandy. It appears that as part of a secret deal Margaret gave up the island in return for French aid - Jean de Carbonel occupied the castle without a fight so it would appear the castle was betrayed. It is around this time that the castle begins to be adapted to accommodate cannon and many of the older towers were adapted to take the new weapons. A document produced in 1462 lists the artillery and the cannon in the castle but this was of no real account for on 17th May 1468 Sir Richard Harliston began a siege which lasted until October when the French garrison surrendered. The castle was not to suffer foreign occupation again until 1940.

In the late 15th century the castle began a transformation into an artillery fortress which during the 16th century saw work on a massive scale in which the builders were continually being outpaced by the development of artillery. The decision was taken to build a new fortress, Elizabeth Castle, in St Aubin's Bay specifically designed as an artillery base and Mont Orgueil, the King's Castle was relegated to le vieux château - the Old Castle. During the 17th century it was used as a political prison for enemies of both Crown and Parliament and in the 1790s it was the base of La Correspondence, a French anti-revolutionary spy network headed by Philippe d'Auvergne. The castle ceased to be a military base in 1907 when it was given to the people of Jersey by the Crown for use as a historic monument.

[2] A Brattice was a wooden housing built on top of the walls. When they were erected on top of towers they were soometimes known as "warheads".

Le Vieux Château

The promontory on which the castle is built was referred to as Gorroic in 1180 by the writer of the Great Roll of the Norman Exchequer while a century later the Extente of 1274 refers to it as Gorryk. The more familiar name of Gorey first appears in the 1330s when French manuscripts refer to the site as Gorri, Gurri and sometimes as le Château de Gouray. For most of the medieval period the castle was simply referred to as Gorey or the King's Castle - it seems to have acquire the rather more romantic title of Mont Orgueil - Mont Pride in the early 15th century traditionally from Thomas, the Duke of Clarence, a brother of Henry V although the first written reference dates from the French occupation of the castle in 1462. Once Elizabeth Castle had been built in the 1590s, it was simply referred to as le Vieux Château.

(31) A detail of Major NVL Rybot's drawing showing sappers using pickaxes to undermine the walls.

(32) Iron heads from pick axes as shown in use above.

(33) A reconstruction of what the Gatehouse at Grosnez Castle may have looked like from the inside by Major NVL Rybot.

Trading and Ships

During the second half of the 12th century the Channel Islands grew in importance as a stopping off point for travellers between the Plantagenet possessions in England and Aquitaine. As trade increased the islands would have been used by all sorts of merchant shipping.

It was during this time that ships in northern waters began to adopt the stern hung rudder, and the old fashioned steering board gradually disappeared. Ships continued to be clinker-built, that is with overlapping planks, as opposed to the more Mediterranean influenced carvel-built tradition of end-on-end planking. It is also about the end of the 12th century that the compass made its appearance although most mariners still followed the old practices of observation. The ships still tended to stay within sight of land which meant that most shipping between England and Gascony would have passed within sight of the Channel Islands and many would have stopped off especially in St Peter Port with its sheltered, deepwater anchorage.

Obviously moving people and goods by sea was quicker, easier and cheaper than by land. King John quickly established that every foreign ship landing in the islands should pay custom dues of one silver mark and that merchants should also pay customs on their cargoes. He excused islanders from this payment - which could be seen as one of the first privileges the islanders received from the new political regime. Ships from the islands traded with England as well as with

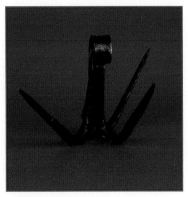

(34) Grappling hook.

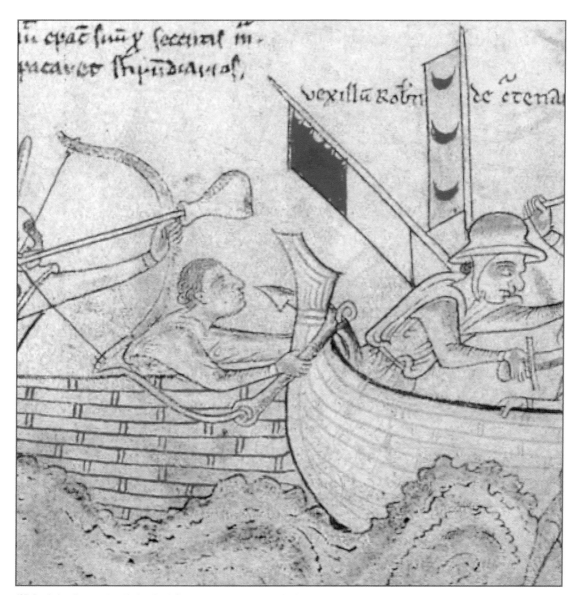

(35) Detail of an illustration from Matthew Paris' 'Chronica Majora' of the Battle of Sandwich showing the use of grappling hooks to secure vessels together in a fight.

Normandy and Brittany and larger ships came from Denmark and Spain. Fish, livestock and canvas was exported and wine and fruit were imported. Because of its position St Peter Port attracted much more trade than Jersey and this can be seen in the amount of customs dues collected in 1331: Guernsey £160, Jersey £9.

In the mid-1980s the remains of a large heavily built vessel were recorded in the harbour at St Peter Port. In the late 1990s more medieval boats were found, the largest of which appears to have been between 25 metres and 30 metres long and planking was up to 28 cms wide and about 41/2 cms thick. They were all built in the Nordic tradition and, judging from the pottery associated with them, appear to have sunk around the end of the thirteenth century.

Although some trading centres built jetties and piers for ships to tie up against or unload, there were no real harbours in the Channel Islands at this time. St Peter Port with its sheltered deep-water anchorage was the most important trade centre in the islands but most sheltered bays could be used. In Jersey St Helier, Rozel, Gorey, (Grève de) Lecq, Bouilly, St Aubin, Bonne Nuit, L'Etac as well as the two mysteriously named Eweries and Waletremble were all named as ports during the 13th century.

(36) Long warships powered by oars similar to this one being built in Denmark, were being built in Jersey in 1241.

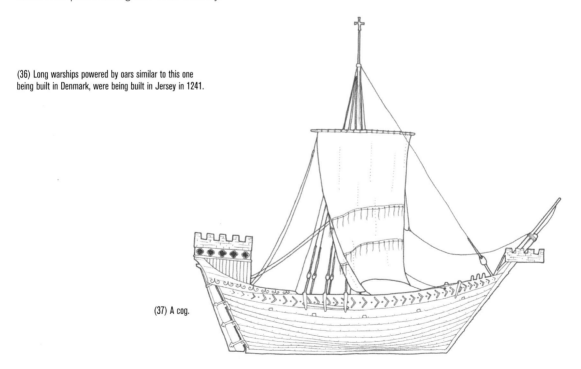

(37) A cog.

Ships

By the 12th century the ocean going Viking cargo boats known as knarrs had developed and were used throughout the Atlantic seaboard. Large beamy, clinker built and driven by a single square sail these undecked vessels could be found in most trading centres. While these continued to be built and traded, a new type of ship began to evolve in the 13th century - these new vessels were known as cogs. They were decked with a flat bottom and were driven by a single square sail. They are usually shown as having a straight stem and stern and with a high freeboard, which meant that they were very roomy, deep vessels with sharp ends. They were heavily built with massive frames and through beams that crossed the width of the hull. The new shape meant that she was better offloaded at a quay and so the stern hung rudder began to replace the side hung steering board. They also had a windlass fitted to help the crew with the heavy work of hoisting sails, hauling the anchor or shifting the cargo. During the middle of the century the largest class carried over 24-tons of cargo, by the 14th century the largest class was described as carrying more than 120-tons.

The cog was used to export wool from England to Flanders and to ship wine from Gascony to England and northern Europe. It was especially popular in the German trading cities known as the Hanseatic League. In 1962 the remains of such a vessel were found in the German city of Bremen which measured 23.5 metres in length, 7 metres in the beam and was able to carry 130-tons of cargo. While they were merchant vessels they were also fitted with fighting platforms - fore-castles and after-castles - because of the ever-present danger poised by pirates. By the 14th century the after-castle grew larger and eventually became accommodation for important passengers and the captain.

(38) Building the replica of the Gedesby boat in Denmark. It is thought that the sunken boats found in St Peter Port harbour would have been like this.

(39) A Hulk.

Later ships

In the late 14th century a different type of clinker-built, decked vessel developed and began operating in these northern waters - the hulk. Most of the evidence for this new category of ship comes from images on seals and manuscript illustrations. They had very rounded bows and stern which were also very high which gave the planking a very pronounced curve. There was no stem or sternpost, instead the planking carried on up instead. The hull was stiffened by through-beams, which were fastened with wooden pegs. The few illustrations that exist show that these vessels often had a hatch in the side to allow easy loading of timber or livestock. For the first time, the single mast is shown with ratlines, which the seamen used to climb to reach the top of the mast. The ends of the single yards from which the sail hung often had hooks attached which could damage any ships that came too close.

Shipbuilding

In 1241 the Warden, Drogo de Barentyn was ordered to have 2 galleys built in the islands and his accounts show that £91 8s 101/2d was paid out for them. In 1244 he was ordered to build an unspecified number of galleys and a covered shelter for them.

We do not know where in the islands these ships were built or what the yard would have looked like. However, in the late 1980s a medieval shipyard site was excavated in Poole, Dorset, which shows that boats were built on slips on the foreshore and that often recycled timbers from older boats were used.

The first recorded ship building site in Jersey was Gorey Castle in 1468 when the French garrison tried to build two small boats.

Further Reading

M. Syvret & J. Stevens
Balleine's History of Jersey
Philimore (1998)

H.M. Bradbury
Philip Augustus - King of France 1180-1223
Longman (1998)

S.D. Church (editor)
King John - New Interpretations
Boydell (1999)

G. Duby
France in the Middle Ages 987-1460
Blackwell (1991)

J.E. Everard & J.C. Holt
Jersey 1204 - The Forging of an Island Community
Thames and Hudson (2004)

E. King
Medieval England
Tempus (2001)

L. James Marr
A History of the Bailiwick of Guernsey
Phillimore (1982)

B. Landström
Sailing Ships
George Allen & Unwin (1978)

J.H. Le Patourel
The Medieval Administration of the Channel Islands
O.U.P. (1937)

N.A.M. Rodgers
The Safeguard of the Sea:
A Naval History of Britain 660-1649
WW Norton & Co (1998)

N.V.L. Rybot
Gorey Castle
States of Jersey (1978)

Picture credits

British Library 1, 15, 19, 21; Centre for Medieval Technology, Denmark 38; City of Bayeux 6,7,8; Master and Fellows of Corpus Christie College, Cambridge 35; Dean and Chapter of Worcester Cathedral 16; Mrs M Finlaison 10; Doug Ford 2, 11, 12, 23, 24, 25, 26, 36; Harnois - Jacques Martel 27, 28; Shaun Heslop 37, 39; Jersey Heritage Trust 9; Musée de Normandie 32, 34; National Antiquities Museum, Stockholm 3, 5; Pierpont Morgan Library, New York 14, 17, 18; Public Record Office, London; 13; Société Jersiaise 4, 20, 22, 29, 31 and 33; Museum of London 40.

The Matrix

Ingelram de Préaux's original matrix from the Museum of London is an extremely rare object dating from the end of the 12th century. The modern wax impression shows how it looked the right way round.

Ingelram went to England and found favour with John I. He signed many charters of donation to various monasteries. He also seems to have moved freely to Normandy where he is recorded as a witness at the courts of justice in 1213.